MW01231549

REWIRE YOUR BRAIN

BUILD MENTAL TOUGHNESS, TRAIN YOUR BRAIN TO INCREASE WILLPOWER

CARL CILLAS

The following Book is reproduced below with the goal of providing information that is as accurate and reliable as possible. Regardless, purchasing this Book can be seen as consent to the fact that both the publisher and the author of this book are in no way experts on the topics discussed within and that any recommendations or suggestions that are made herein are for entertainment purposes only. Professionals should be consulted as needed prior to undertaking any of the action endorsed herein.

This declaration is deemed fair and valid by both the American Bar Association and the Committee of Publishers Association and is legally binding throughout the United States.

Furthermore, the transmission, duplication, or reproduction of any of the following work including specific information will be considered an illegal act irrespective of if it is done electronically or in print. This extends to creating a secondary or tertiary copy of the work or a recorded copy and is only allowed with the express written consent from the Publisher. All additional right reserved.

The information in the following pages is broadly considered a truthful and accurate account of facts and as such, any inattention, use, or misuse of the information in question by the reader will render any resulting actions solely under their purview. There are no scenarios in which the publisher or the original author of this work can be in any fashion deemed liable for any hardship or damages that may befall them after undertaking information described herein.

Additionally, the information in the following pages is intended only for informational purposes and should thus be thought of as universal. As befitting its nature, it is presented without assurance regarding its prolonged validity or interim quality. Trademarks that are mentioned are done without written consent and can in no way be considered an endorsement from the trademark holder.

TABLE OF CONTENTS

Introduction

Do you believe that everything happens for a reason? I do. I believe that what you need will always find its way to you. You picked up this book for a reason. Something is missing in your life, something that your soul is longing for. Something bigger and wildly abundant that is waiting for you right around the corner. The only thing standing between you and whatever that "something" is, is you, or, more specifically, your mindset.

This book is going to help you identify and transform the limiting beliefs that are blocking you from all the abundant possibilities that await you so that you can get serious about what you want and take action toward making it happen. Don't worry; I'm going to give you the tools you need to do it all with ease.

I'm excited and honored to travel along on this journey with you. My greatest wish is that the information in this book is as transformational for you as it has been for me, and the many people I've had the privilege of sharing it with.

You might be wondering what kind of an impact this will really make on your life. All I can say is this: just try it! Give it a good, honest and consistent effort. Once you start to feel a shift in your energy, you'll get to witness your desires begin to manifest right before your eyes and start to see what can only be described as miracles happening everywhere.

I wasn't always a believer. In fact, I was a big-time skeptic of mindset work at first. It all sounded a little too "woo" to me. So, if you're in the same camp, wondering if this is going to work for you, this book is a perfect introduction, as there is a healthy balance of practicality throughout. I promise not to go too woo on you!

If, however, you've been on the mindset bandwagon for a while, this book is going to help you take your practice to the next level and beyond. That's because I take everything you already know about positive mindset and the Laws of Attraction and Vibration and put it into a repeatable system you can implement again and again to get the results you want.

Whether you're a mindset newbie or a seasoned vet, you'll find a tremendous amount of value in this book, and I look forward to helping you ditch your limits and take control of the life you've been dreaming about and totally deserve.

While your vision board can be a huge source of inspiration and motivation it can also be a compass of sorts. Sometimes it can be all too easy to get so caught up in the motions of pursuing a goal that you lose track of the destination itself. This can result in you making less progress than you imagine, or even worse, making some choices along the way that serve to take you further away from your goal rather than closer to it. By constantly reminding yourself of where it is you are trying to get you can better judge whether or not you are actually going in the right direction.

Another way that your vision board can help keep you going in the right direction is by showing you the changes you need for success. Sometimes you might find that you have a behavior or a mindset that undermines your efforts, thereby standing between you and the success you desire. Whenever you identify such an obstacle you can put something on your vision board to encourage you to overcome it. Any inspirational quotes or motivational writings that address the things you are trying to overcome will give you the strength you need to make those necessary changes in your life.

Cheers to a mind-blowing journey,

Self-Limiting Mindset and How to Increase Willpower

Self-discipline is a skill - one that can be learned like riding a bike. Learn self-discipline as if you're trying to learn to ride a bike or swim in the ocean – it takes time to cultivate the skill. If you don't know how to swim, how do you start? You dip in the water and start practicing. Then you stay afloat for a while and repeat until you can swim. You build the momentum to practice more until you're a swimmer. Self-discipline is based on 2 things: daily practice and momentum. To obtain self-discipline, a person has to hone their skills to build consistency and small step their way until they've mastered the skill.

Why does a person need self-discipline? The answer: to achieve what's hard. To give up your bad habits, to perform at your job, to achieve your goals –discipline is required. Self-discipline can be trained like any other habit; the key to success is perseverance. Once you strengthen your self-discipline, you'll be able to do things in life such as get rid of your bad habits, increase your productivity, become fit and happy. Self-discipline is hard - as its re-shapes your mind to go beyond your basic emotional needs.

3 Habits That Build Self-Discipline

Pro Tip: To obtain self-discipline, treat your brain as if you're an athlete and you need daily training to compete in the sport championship. What happens when an athlete misses their daily training? They fall out of shape. Give yourself time if you're just starting and kick yourself in the butt when you're slacking.

The following are the #3 essential skills to develop a self-discipline mindset:

1) The "One Day to Success" Habit

The self-discipline mindset is managed on the macro: You have to prepare your brain for the long-term, but act in small daily increments. The #1 technique to obtain self-discipline what we call the "One day to success" habit:

- The 1-Day to Success Habit: "If you did it for one day, treat yourself as if you're already successful."

If you stick to your diet for one day, be as happy as if you've already lost weight. Don't wait until you have a shiny 6-pack to give yourself a pat on the back. Long-term success is built on small daily success and it makes sense to celebrate once you've gone through a full day of discipline. Measure your success based on what you've done in a day – if you've successfully disciplined yourself, treat yourself as if you already achieved your goal. Did you do your work today? If you completed your tasks, act as if you're already at the finish line. Base your self-esteem and happiness on your daily set of tasks, and if you complete them – consider yourself a successful person.

This is a mind shift that will get your mind to build momentum by acting as if you made it once you've gone through a full day of self-discipline. Large successes are built on daily milestones. The wrong approach is to wait for 30 days or 6 months until you reward yourself and say you've "made it" – the right approach is to discipline yourself for a day and then pat yourself on the back for your accomplishments that day. If you did it for a day – consider yourself successful. If you failed to do it – try again tomorrow.

2) Kill Instant Gratification

Human nature wires us to consume things that provide us immediate gratification: Bad foods, alcohol, cigarettes, the news, movies, social media - what do these all have in common? They provide instant emotional relief & gratification. Self-discipline is the art of optimizing your mind for delayed, long-term gratification. If you eat the candy bar immediately which you know you're not supposed to eat you'll be gratified instantly. If you say no to the candy and consume broccoli instead, you'll get a better body in 30 days – the difference is that you'll be gratified later. Discipline is different from self-control because in self-control we exercise restraint, while with self-discipline we essentially re-wire our brain for discipline for the long term.

Self-discipline is a life-long task that challenges our mind continually, on a daily basis - accept that as long as you're alive, your mind will always push you to take the way of instant gratification – that's your biology following a survival instinct. We always want to eat because back when we used to live in tribes, if we didn't eat, we'd die. We always want to have sex because if we didn't, we wouldn't reproduce. We are addicted to substances and social media because they ping our brain with dopamine chemicals that signal, we're safe. The key is not to change our biology, but to observe it objectively and take control of it.

Pro Tip: Become God. Imagine yourself as God watching your room from above. To beat our biology, we have to observe our impulsive behaviors from a 3rd person perspective: Where are you at right now? You're in a room, you are reading a book. If you go to the kitchen, observe your behavior. Ask yourself – is this person doing something rational, or are they acting primitive? Take control of your bad behavior by removing your identity from your actions and looking at yourself through the prism of a neutral entity.

3) Create Momentum Waves

Once you've achieved your daily success, repeat the same process by pushing through your daily milestones. This will create "Momentum Waves" that you ride like a surfer catching a wave in the open ocean – you find a big wave and you catch it; you fall off and climb back on. If you exercise for 1 day, repeat your actions diligently for a week. This will create huge momentum for you to keep going for a full month. Once you've done it for a month, keep going for a full year.

4 Essential Practices to Ignite Strong Willpower

What do you do when you "don't feel like doing it"? How do you find the energy to go to the gym at night when you feel like sleeping and staying inside? How do you get up at 5am to go prepare for work when you want an extra hour of sleep? How do you get the motivation to do those things you're supposed to, and do them consistently? The answer is willpower. Willpower can be the deciding factor between a successful goal and a failed goal.

What is the difference between a millionaire CEO who runs his own company and a homeless person on the street? The difference is willpower. One has the willpower to push through and be successful, while the other one lacks willpower and can barely function in life. Some people want to be successful, and they know what it takes to be successful - but they lack the willpower to do it.

Willpower is a muscle – it's the muscle in that brain that is weak when left untrained - if you do nothing to practice your willpower, you will slack and be unproductive. Treat your brain as a vehicle and willpower as the motor: If you don't have a motor, or if you have a half-functioning motor you won't be able to drive the vehicle. However, if the motor is well-oiled and the mechanics are functioning - you'll be able to drive your vehicle through the roughest terrain in the mountains. The same applies for your brain - when you have willpower, you have a functioning brain that will get you to do anything. Want to be able to wake up at 5AM and feel great? Want to be able to exercise at night and look forward to your trip to the gym? Want to be able to work 10 hours without breaks or distractions? Fix your willpower – and you can achieve it.

Willpower has to be built gradually - one doesn't develop willpower overnight. Be careful not to be too overwhelmed, even if the goals seem realistic. For example, if your goal is to exercise at 9PM sharp every night makes sure that you don't burn yourself out too much or you might not be able to exercise tomorrow. Take breaks and reward yourself once every few days, in order to not burn out. Start by taking small increments, and build your willpower using the techniques below gradually. Once you gain momentum, continue doing it and the actions will become a part of your identity.

Remember the 6-month rule: What seemed hard for you to do today will become an average day for you in 6 months. If you thought running and lifting weights in one day is impossible, once you get yourself to do it once - you might find this is an average day for you after 6 months; and you'll add another activity on top. Your willpower will peak after your brain has evidence it's possible. To give it evidence, you must throw yourself in the line of fire every day. You will naturally have dips in the process, and you must pick yourself up. Once your momentum dips, force yourself to do it again and your willpower will peak.

1) Give Your Brain Proof, Not Promises

Remember this phrase: "Your brain wants proof - not promises". Your brain works like a coin machine: Once it's given proof it can do it; it gives willpower in return. If you tell yourself "I will eat better today", your brain won't notice and give you the willpower to do it. However, if you force yourself to do it - you cook healthy food and consume it; your brain will have definite proof that it's possible. Then, it will naturally

—

provide you the willpower to repeat it the next day. Your brain is in constant demand for proof that you can do certain things, and you must feed it physical proof if you want to get the willpower in return.

2) Start with Uncomfortable Tasks

What happens when you start work in the morning? You feel discomfort. What happens when you start jogging on the track? You feel discomfort. What happens when you go for a job interview? You feel discomfort. Discomfort is what you need – it means the action is worth pursuing. Now think about what happens when you push through discomfort - you become comfortable with the habit and you start engaging with it. The discomfort you're feeling in this case is not caused by lack of ideal circumstance – it's caused by your own biological resistance. Biological resistance tries to chain you in place and conserve energy; therefore, you must do the opposite of what you're feeling inside your body.

3) Give 100% Effort in Every Task

Willpower is not only about starting - it's about finishing your tasks at 100% diligence. How do you develop the willpower to do a task, if not by giving your best? The wrong approach is to start an uncomfortable task and slack through, thinking that by delaying the task you can still get it done another day. The right approach is to work as if your life depends on it. Imagine someone put a gun to your head and told you - "Go out to the gym and do 150 pushups, lift 5 reps and run 10 miles". Would you find the willpower to do it? You definitely would, as your life is under threat.

4) Cut Off Distractions

Remove all distractions that restrain you from completing your work. Once you've gone through an hour or two of work, you'll feel tempted to take a break and indulge in "relaxation" periods. The downside to this is that it's usually more distractions that arise once you discover one distraction. If you're scrolling on Instagram, you'll find your ex posting something that makes you emotional or an ad that encourages you to travel to Bali.

Clarify Your Vision and the Importance of Willpower in Life

Understanding Willpower and the Benefits You Can Gain from Having It

It is important to understand what willpower is and its impact on how you live your life. Only with this kind of understanding will you be able to take advantage of its benefits.

What is will?

Will is your ability to make conscious choices. Humans have free will and can make their own choices; it doesn't matter if it conforms to other people's concepts or commands. You can relate will to desire. If you don't want something, you won't have the will to achieve it. On the other hand, having a strong desire for something you want to achieve, you are going to persist until you realize it, no matter what. Remember the old adage if there's a will, there's a way?

What is willpower?

Willpower is your ability to control unnecessary and harmful impulses. It is your motivation to exercise will. Psychologists define willpower as your ability to delay gratification and resist short-term temptations to meet your long-term goals.

It is an intangible human force that empowers you to attain whatever goals and dreams you have despite encountering disheartening doubts or great adversity. More often than not, willpower makes up for your lack of education, talent, or ability; and conversely, the absence of willpower makes you give up the moment you encounter even the slightest hurdle.

When there is willpower, you also have to have self-discipline. It gives you the drive to persevere. Self-discipline gives you the ability to face and withstand the challenges and adversities you have to face, whether they are physical, mental, or emotional difficulties.

What are the benefits of having willpower and self-discipline?

You need both willpower and self-discipline to control your thoughts, so you become the boss of your own mind. A strong willpower and self-discipline give you more power over your thoughts and feelings, thus giving you more power to concentrate and focus on something that you want to achieve.

Being a master of your own mind gives you inner peace. While you may encounter events that do not go in you favor, your inner peace is not disturbed because these negative things do not affect your thoughts and your feelings.

With willpower, you can sway criticisms and hurdles to your advantage. It serves as your springboard to hone your skills and craft. It serves as your motivation to get past these difficulties and emerge victorious. Your will to survive and withstand adversity will help propel you to overcome and you become virtually unstoppable.

Willpower and self-discipline will be helpful if you want to change bad habits. It gives you more control over your desires.

Eliminate Barriers to Your Willpower Success Such as Perfectionism and Self-Doubt

To succeed in developing strong willpower, you have to first defeat two destructive enemies: perfectionism and self-doubt. You have to know who you are and come to terms with what you are capable of. Do not underrate yourself by thinking that you are working with imperfections. There is nothing wrong with striving to achieve perfection. It takes a strong willpower and confidence to do so.

Dealing with Perfectionism

Perfectionism can be destructive to your life in ways that you can think:

Perfectionism defeats your initiative. You might have an important project that you need to work on, but you don't know how to begin. You keep on saying to yourself that you'll soon begin once you've got the right time for it or once you have the money to spend. With losing weight, maybe you cannot begin because you want the perfect timing, like when you have the time and money to enroll in a fitness center. This is killing your goal because your standards are so high.

It can destroy your relationships. Sometimes perfectionism can be rooted in insecurity.

It robs you of your happiness. You become your worst critic, so everything that you do is never good enough.

Eliminating barriers to enhance your willpower is important. Follow these tips to control perfectionism:

Forgive yourself. Keep in mind that nobody's perfect and you have your own strengths and weaknesses. There is always something new to learn so just keep on learning but don't be too hard on yourself.

Maintain your focus on your specific goals. What is your real purpose for pursuing you goal? Is it to be perfect or you wanted something to get done? Perfectionism hinders you from getting timely results because you always wait for the perfect time to begin and it often leads you procrastinate.

Create SMART goals.

Do not mix results with judgment. When you work on a project, do not think about how your colleagues will perceive the overall result, a perfectionist thinks that way. Eat healthy and exercise to get fit and not just for simple weight targets.

Learn from critics. Listen to your critics but do not take them personally. You can learn a thing or two from them. Work to improve not to gain approval.

Get started. Don't wait for the right conditions because they will never come. Even if you are unsure yet, you have to start somewhere. You might be surprised that the barriers you have imagined you might encounter are not that difficult after all.

Set a deadline. Even if it is just a self-imposed deadline, you should make it anyway because it gives you a sense of purpose and gets you started. If a goal is too overwhelming, break it down into smaller pieces to make them easier to handle.

Learn from your mistakes. You are not perfect and when you make mistakes, you have to accept and learn from them. Reflect on the failures but you shouldn't dwell on them for so long. Begin again armed with what you have learned from your mistakes.

Reflect on your successes. Remember the things that you have successfully done in the past. See how far you have become with all your flaws and weaknesses. Instead of trying to do a few things perfectly, try to accomplish a lot of things successfully.

Take these techniques to heart and soon you'll be enhancing your willpower.

Believing in Yourself

Another barrier that hinders you from exercising your willpower is self-doubt. When there is a task in front of you, you might initially think that you can't do it and that it is too difficult for you. Thinking that you're going to fail anyway, so you don't attempt to do it and the voice inside you tells you that you are never good enough.

These are the things that you need to do to erase self-doubt:

Recognize your doubts. The moment you hear yourself say that you cannot do it, or you worry about failing, immediately turn these negative self-talks into positive. So, the next time you hear yourself say, "What if I can't do it and fail miserably?" respond by saying, "It's okay to fail because I can always try again."

Do not listen to "toxic" people. These are the people who always say and notice the negative things. Do not listen to them because they will just flood your thoughts with self-doubt. Associate yourself with people who will lift you up.

Remember your previous accomplishments. When you begin to doubt your abilities, think about the times you succeeded. Keep a list of your accomplishments, no matter how small they are. Each time you feel self-doubt creeps in, bring out your list and go over them to remind you what you can really do.

Learn to trust and love yourself. Before you expect other people to love you, you have to love yourself first. You have to be your own supporter first. Be kind to yourself.

Give yourself a chance to try and try again. Realize that self-doubt will always be there, you just have to learn to deal with it. It's a fact that there will always be instances that you will fail, but you have to forgive yourself for not being perfect and make failures challenge you to try and try again until you get things right.

Perfectionism and self-doubt rob you of true success because they block off motivation, drive, and willpower. Practice these techniques and see your life improve.

How to Develop Mental Toughness

At the very core of mental toughness is consistency. Once you create a goal, consistently striving toward it every day, one step at a time, is what going to earn you grits. If you're an artist or want to be, that looks like creating something, even if it's small, every single day without failing. If you're an athlete, it looks like showing up early to practice every single time, completely focused and ready to go, and never missing a workout. If you're a nurse, it looks like showing up for your patients, even when you're tired, in any form they need you to be.

The great news about mental toughness is this: you can have it. That voice in your head, that's been telling you someone else deserves your dreams because they're just more talented or have better skills than you, are wrong. Talent and genetics can be completely overrun by one person who has the drive and the willpower to focus hard on getting where they want to be. Anyone can achieve mental toughness. That anyone includes you.

Being mentally tough means, you'll be better prepared for change. It means you'll be more positive under pressure, more productive during the workday, and harness more emotional stability. It means you'll grow into the part of yourself that believes your happiness has nothing to do with your external world and everything to do with your internal world.

Being mentally tough means, you'll focus on your goals and dreams instead of just reacting to life as it comes. You'll be more patient with the outcomes because you can see clearly how you're getting there, and you'll experience a more relaxed, content countenance. All of this can be yours. Are you ready to begin?

Be a self-starter

Motivation is at the root of mental strength. Those considered to be mentally tough usually show what sports psychologists refer to as the' inherent' motive. This is defined by a research carried out in Psychology of motor behavior. People who are inherently motivated are self-starters who are prepared to push hard for the love of what they do and want to accomplish. They need little encouragement to do their best and often set their own objectives. This does not happen to all of us, of course. Some people can only get their heads into a match if the rivalry is under pressure. They thrive at the opportunity to compare themselves with others.

Remain positive

Your mind is on a dialog every day whether you realize it or not. The thinking generally combines outside stimuli with your own views about yourself. Some of them are going to be negative, but in order to succeed, you must concentrate on those that make you feel better. It sounds like heartfelt advice, but you would find it difficult to find a successful individual who does not practice this.

Get uncomfortable

You cannot be comfortable with a routine that constantly gets your down and expects to go far. If you are attempting to be more mentally tough, you need to exercise the brain little longer or more quickly than you are accustomed to a couple of times a month. The mental toughness training sessions should be random just like wearing your running shoes one day and deciding to challenge your running or jogging limits.

Always be prepared

Think about any issues that might occur and come up with a solution. For instance, during the triathlon, challenges would be something like; flat bicycle pneumatics, your glasses can be shot while you're swimming or getting blistered. It will be mentally helpful if you know that you have done all you can to reach your objective by being prepared to deal with challenges that arise along the way.

Maintain a trusted inner circle

A trusted inner circle is not just a group of people you believe cannot betray you by putting your dirty laundry out in the public. If you want to be successful and above all develop mental toughness, it is crucial that you have a group of the trusted inner circle that challenges you to be a better version of yourself.

Building Consistency

To excel at training your body to develop your mental toughness, you must be consistent. It is consistency in working out and getting in shape that separates those who reach their ultimate fitness or weight loss goals from those who lose a few pounds and build a bit of muscle and then give up. Consistency causes that connection to keep on moving, doing boot camp and fitness training, instead of collapsing in the field.

Small Wins Pay Off!

One of the most important ideas to remember is that small wins pay off. Every time you excel at doing something better than you did before or go further than you thought you could, you are building the mental toughness it takes to transform your life.

Neutralizing Toxic People's Effects on You

When we are constantly worried about what other people are thinking, it can be easy for your self-confidence to plummet. It can also affect how you face your fears, overcome obstacles, and ultimately achieve the success that you have set out to accomplish. When you are mentally tough, you have the ability to neutralize the toxic effect that people can have on you. Instead of becoming mentally and emotionally exhausted from people like this, once you have mastered mental toughness you will find that it is easier for you to stop feeding into their negative ways.

Embracing Change

Change is inevitable, and it will happen in all areas of your life. From personal matters to work problems, there is going to be change. Perhaps there will be a change in routine, a change in goals, a change in your ability to reach your goals, a change in plans that you thought were already set in stone, or any other number of changes. Regardless of what has inspired these changes, they are bound to happen. People who lack resilience and mental toughness struggle with change. It is hard for them to adapt when things go off course. They often get frustrated and feel uncomfortable, as though they have lost their direction and their ability to navigate the new map.

Saying No

If you are not great at saying no, there is only one real way to get better at it. That is, practice. Start practicing by saying no to small things or to people who are less important than those that you feel a genuine sense of obligation toward. The easier it gets, the more you can say no to bigger things and more important people. Eventually, you will find it much easier to say no to the people you feel obligated to. Keep practicing and remember to honor your boundaries. You are not wrong for having them, nor should you feel guilty for honoring them. In fact, doing so is a very clear sign of mental strength.

Manage Stress

You know stress when you feel it. The source of stress can be psychosocial, physical, or psychological. You feel threatened by the situation you're facing and doubt your ability to handle it successfully. Severe stress causes fatigue and burnout. We become disillusioned, pessimistic, and cynical. The body is programmed to handle immediate stressful situations by choosing either to fight or to run away.

Embracing Failure and Refraining from Dwelling

You are going to fail. Everyone is going to fail. It is a fact of life. Or, it isn't. That is, not if you don't want it to be. Here's the thing, you are not going to reach your goal the first time, every single time you set out to achieve one. Perhaps your goal is to open a company and you open one, but it fails and closes within a year, for example. You can look at this experience in one of two ways: one, you failed and did not meet your goal. Or, two, you opened a company successfully and learned many valuable lessons along the way that you can use toward future endeavors. In the first example, you have failed. In the second, however, you have learned a lesson.

Practicing Self-Care

When you genuinely take care of yourself and your needs, physically, mentally, and spiritually, it becomes a lot easier for you to endure the inevitable parts of life. Stress, inconveniences, fear, and other hardships all become a lot easier to manage when you are feeling at peace inside. When you are at war with yourself and you are letting your own wellbeing fall short, your mind, body, and soul all struggle to manage daily wild cards. Caring for yourself maximizes your resiliency towards life.

Learn from mistakes and let it go

When you commit a mistake, you should see it as a chance to learn something new. Your mistakes don't define you. Think of how you're going to make sure that next time, you will know how to ensure everything goes right. If a loved one or another person makes mistakes, you should also see it as a chance to be understanding, kind, and forbearing.

Impress yourself

You can't please everyone and while people may like your clothes, title or possessions, that doesn't mean that they really like you. What you want to have is a genuine relationship with the people around you. This can only be achieved when you start trying to be yourself and stop trying to please others. You will have the more mental energy for those who really care about you.

Tweak Your Self-Talk

Tweaking your self-talk towards positivity sounds easy and straightforward enough, but so many of us have negative self-talk already programmed into our brains as a habit. You have to rewire yourself to think positively. Start by coming up with truthful affirmations for moments of panic and anxiety. Pessimism tends to tell you that bad things last forever, are universal, and mean you're a horrible person.

Mental Toughness - High Frustration Tolerance

Would we change who we are, what we feel, and also how we behave? Can a leopard change its spots? I recently talked to somebody who asked if a psychologist is just painting over the spots of the "leopard," and underneath, we all stay the same. Okay, I don't see many leopards in my consultation room, but I see people still shifting. A positively changed mind-set is important for cognitive strength and resilience. Read on, and I will continue to discuss this issue.

The fundamental difference between a leopard, a dog, a tree, and a human being is that other living things have already figured out their course and purpose. A leopard will become a leopard; a tree will do what a leopard does. The manual for directions is included.

It is our duty to us human beings, who and what we are in every moment. We are self-conscious and self-determined. We are dropped into the world with no script or stage directions as actors on a stage. We don't have a manual of instructions. That is why our responsibility is who we are and what we become. Of course, there are factors that affect who we are today and which I have mentioned below, but the important point I am trying to make in this regard is that these factors cannot be overused as excuses for our future.

It is our duty to us human beings, who and what we are in every moment. We are self-conscious and self-determined. We are dropped into the world with no script or stage directions as actors on a stage. We don't have a manual of instructions. That is why our responsibility is who we are and what we become. Of course, there are factors that affect who we are today and which I have mentioned below, but the important point I am trying to make in this regard is that these factors cannot be overused as excuses for our future.

Set Smart Goals

Sometimes we are not able to achieve our goals or are able to create new habits because we have certain emotional issues that get in our way. Whether it be due to certain mental health issues, or simply a sensitivity, reacting to your emotions is a habit in itself, one that is learned, and can easily be unlearned.

Feeling emotional is not a bad thing. It is only when our emotions are left unchecked and unexpressed that they begin to interfere with our daily activities and goals. There are many ways that you can learn how to more regulate your emotions in a healthier manner, but before we get to that, we will discuss the importance of self-care and various relaxation techniques

The Importance of Self-Care

Various studies within the past few years have learned the importance of self-care and how it affects our productivity and performances in life. What self-care is essential, is the time that we take to relax and participate in activities and hobbies that we enjoy.

It can be things like getting a massage, getting your nails done, or it can anything as simple as scheduling time to watch a good movie. Here is a list of the various benefits of self-care on your mental and physical health, as well as various reasons as to why integrating self-care into your life is important:

- Knowing Your Worth: Self-care reminds you that maintaining a healthy relationship with yourself produces positive feels and boosts your confidence and self-esteem. It also tells you that your needs and desires are as important as others.

- A Healthy Work-Life Balance: Contrary to what many people believe, over-working is not a virtue. Accompanying this activity is an unhealthy amount of stress, less productivity, and disorganized emotional development. Overworking can lead to all kinds of mental and physical health problems, such as anxiety and depression, insomnia, and heart disease. Self-care can range from activities outside of work to ones at work, such as making sure you take your breaks, avoiding overextending, and setting professional boundaries.

- Stress Management: Constant stress and anxiety is incredibly unhealthy. There is such a thing as a normal amount of stress because it can inspire you to achieve your goals and move forward. Self-care helps you recharge your batteries and allows you to face your goals in a more relaxed and productive manner.

- Start Living, Stop Existing: Everyone has a lot of responsibilities, which means they are things that we have to do in life. They are not always things that we enjoy, such as paying bills, fixing the dryer, and doing the dishes, but once we take the time for self-care, we realize that self-care is also a responsibility. Taking the time for things you enjoy helps you get up in the morning and have things to look forward to when there are a lot of things in life that we have to do.

- Better Physical Health: Your physical health will benefit while your mental health does because you have made the choice to participate in physical exercise, eat better, get a good amount of sleep, and take care of your hygiene.

You don't have to be a monk and sit for hours on end in order to receive the various benefits that come with deep relaxation and meditation. Take about 20 minutes out of your day and try to note how you are feeling both before, and after. Certain techniques may appeal to you more than others, so feel free to go over a few of them more than once in order to find what suits you.

Relaxed Breath Techniques

The point of breathing exercises and relaxation strategies is not to replace the sensation of anxiety, depression or anger, or to run from it, but to embrace it, and help you learn the difference between thoughts and physical sensations. These strategies will help you become more aware of how your body reacts to certain thoughts and moods. Please take note of when you feel you may be using one of those strategies in order to flee from the unpleasant feeling. This is not the point of them and will only injure your progress in the long run.

Breathing Exercises: Slow Diaphragmatic Breathing

This technique sends a direct signal to the brain to let it know that it is safe. This practice is usually recommended to be done alone, either before you start your day or after it. You can apply it while you are in a situation that makes you anxious or are coping with memory or triggered depressive thoughts. But remember, you are not doing this to rid yourself of the anxiety. If you are doing it at the moment, remember that it is meant to have the emotion felt, and to remind you that you are safe.

From a comfortable chair with your feet on the floor or find a place to lie down.

Place your hands onto your belly and allow them to rest gently.

Start by observing your breath. Try not to judge the pace in which your belly is rising and falling.

Begin filling up your belly with an inhale slow, so it starts to feel like a little beach ball or globe. Imagine a balloon being filled up. Do not do this roughly or too fast. Focus on breathing into your stomach, and not allowing your shoulders to lift as you inhale.

Breathe out slowly to the count of five. Try to do this as slowly as possible.

After the exhale, hold for about 2-3 seconds before you inhale into your belly again.

Breathe in and out this way and observe how your breath has slowed down.

Practice this for around 10 minutes.

This practice will work better if you try to do this twice a day at the beginning of your treatment. Try to do it at the same point of the day, every day. This is usually a good start for those who suffer from anxiety or anger issues.

Progressive Muscle Relaxation

Many people with anxiety, depression and anger issues suffer from muscle tension. For the person with anxiety, it is because when they experience the emotion of that anxiety in their body, their muscle tense up, as a reaction toward a perceived threat (to either participate in fight or flight). People with repressed anger issues suffer from the same problem. Those with depression are known to possess extra tense muscles because of the constant ruminating that causes immense stress within their bodies.

For whatever reason it may be, this technique attempts to employ the opposite. It is the absence of tension in the body's muscles. The aim of it is to gradually learn to release tension in the muscles through daily exercise. This shows your body during moments of anxiety and/or anger that you are safe and reduces the likelihood of a flight or fight response.

The practice has you systematically tensing and relaxing certain muscle groups of the body. If you try it out for a moment and tense your bicep now, for about 5-7 seconds, then allow it to relax, you feel the instant difference in the lack of tension.

Mindfulness: The Benefits

Mindfulness is a practice that has grown in popularity and is often integrated into various forms of therapeutic treatment. Mindfulness is defined as a practice that longs to keep you in the present moment without the desire to flee from whatever feeling, bodily sensation, or behavioral issue may be plaguing you. Many mental health issues thrive on either dwelling on the past or obsessing over the future. Mindfulness practices help you learn to observe your thoughts without judgment or criticism and to teach you how to begin cultivating compassion toward yourself and your experiences.

Mindfulness Meditation

Mindfulness meditation is not just meant for monks. Many people misunderstand what the point of mindful meditation is. An image of someone hovering over the clouds on a mountaintop is a commonly associated misconception. Mindfulness meditation is not practice meant for an elect few. It is meant to be practice by anyone and everyone, no matter what age or point they are in their lives. No matter how busy, stressed, anxious, angry, or unhappy you may be, mindfulness meditation will act as another tool to integrate into your self-care toolbox. It has been successful to help people in the past reduce stress, anxiety, depression, and anger issues.

Depending on what kind of mindfulness meditation you are participating in, the practice will help you by focusing your attention either on a single repetitive action, such as breathing or encourage you to observe a specific portion of your mind. Some practices ask you to observe your thoughts without judgment or criticism, so you can learn that thoughts are just as they are; not you at all. It can also be applied to several activities that involve movement, such as walking, eating, or exercising.

Here is a simple exercise of mindful meditation that you can begin practicing now:

Find a quiet, comfortable space where you know you will not be interrupted or distracted.

Sit on a chair that is straight-backed or sit crossed legged on the floor.

Choose a point of focus; most people like to focus on their breathing at first. It can be the sensation of air moving in and out of your nostrils, your belly rising and falling, or a candle flame or meaningful word you repeated through the practice.

Distracting thoughts do not mean you are 'doing it wrong'. Your mind is like a monkey and is meant to be playing around. If you find yourself becoming distracted, do not be angry. The point is to simply bring your attention back to the selected focus of attention; no matter how many times your mind tries to run off.

Visualization

This is a guided imagery practice and a variation on tradition mediation that involves the imagining of a scene that helps you to feel calm. Each person will have a different scene that makes them feel calm; it can be a beach, a childhood home, or even just your bed at home. You can do visualization either on your own or with a therapist. Aids such as soothing music help some people visualize better, along with sounds that co-inside with your particular location.

Here is an easy visualization exercise that can help you get started:

Close your eyes. Be sure to do this in a place where you are not distracted or unsafe.

Find music, sounds, or rhythmic tones that will help your experience feel more authentic. These can be found through YouTube, or through a simple google search.

Picture your peaceful place as vividly as you can; make note of the sounds, sights, smells, feels, and tastes.

Some people lose track of where they are during a visualization, have heavy limbs, or begin yawning. If this happens to you, don't worry, it is a very common reaction.

If you are unsure as to which practice may benefit you most, try utilizing one day for the following week. You will then begin to notice which ones you feel more comfortable practicing or receive the most benefits from.

Remember, that relaxed breathing techniques and visualization are not practices that are meant to be cure-alls for your mental health issues. They are one part of many building blocks that are going to help you understand your own unique mental health experience.

Other Behavioral Activities

There following are other forms of behavioral activities that can help you better organize and schedule your life, so your emotions can feel further regulated.

Simple Daily Practices to Overcome Procrastination

When talking about procrastination, everyone might relate to it because there isn't anyone who could deny it. At least, once or twice in your life, procrastination would have played its role. Whenever you miss your deadlines, the level of anxiety rises above your head and you are forced to complete the project as soon as possible. But deep down, you know it is impossible to complete because there is so much to do. Yet, you try! Procrastination will make your life miserable, so try not to make it a habit.

Some people want to stop procrastinating, but they are unable to because they don't know how to do it. Or sometimes, they might be missing the motivation they need. And it can be frustrating, I know. You must understand the fact that procrastinating factors differ from one individual to another:

A writer will procrastinate on the project he/she was assigned. And then, he/she must workday and night to complete the project.

A student will delay schoolwork and then, complete it at the last moment.

An athlete will delay medications because they are so concerned about the current game.

If you evaluate each example above, you will understand that through procrastination every individual mentioned in the example will be affected. For instance, the athlete will have to deal with a lot of severe issues if he/she doesn't treat the injury right away. Likewise, there will be a lot of emotional drawbacks as well.

I am going to share some of the practical daily practices that you can follow to overcome procrastination. These practices will help you beat procrastination even if you are feeling lazy or unmotivated. Before you begin reading the practices below, you must bear in mind that you can select any of them. This means you are not forced to perform all the habits below. Let's get started!

1. Find solutions to potential emergencies

Procrastination is not just simply a bad habit; rather it is a dangerous one. It will have a huge impact on your health. Sometimes, you might even lose the great bonds that you shared with your family members. They might even come to a point where they assume that you no longer care. There will be situations in life where you have to deal with unexpected priorities such as death, sickness, and much more. Such situations can't wait because you will have to address them immediately. In such an instance, you would have to drop all the scheduled tasks. Some other times, great family events might turn into dreadful situations, and you can't avoid them and get back to your work. Emergencies don't come with a warning, so you have to put up with the obstacles they create. How can you avoid emergencies? Are you going to stop everything and address the issue? Or if you have already delayed the work and then, something urgent comes up, how are you planning to handle it? What might happen when you ignore the emergencies?

To handle emergencies, you have to have a clear picture of the type of emergencies that you are dealing with. You can think about the aftereffects of avoiding the emergency. Or think about the people who are related to the emergency, how will they feel if you ignore it? What are the actions that you can take to solve this sudden issue so that you can get back to work? Or can you put off the emergency issue because it is not life-threatening?

Before you dig in further, let me tell you. If you are working so hard that you don't even have time for your family, it means you are losing a lot of good things in life, there is a lack of balance. You are not living your life — this where the concept of smart working comes into the picture. You can easily get busy and forget about the people around you. Or you can easily put off emergencies that you believe are not important, and those emergencies might actually turn into severe situations. Of course, you might be so busy that you don't even have time for important things, but it is all about your priorities.

No project, appointment, or meeting is worth ignoring for the emergencies that might affect the life of a loved one. I'd suggest stopping other things when something urgent comes up because procrastination is not only about work but also about life. If you address emergencies right away, you won't have to deal with the worst cases down the line.

Most of the time, we think procrastination is all about work and how we delay work. But I hope I have pointed out something that you should also consider.

If you organize work-related activities and complete them before the deadline, or if you have completed half the work already, unexpected priorities might not create a huge impact on your work life. What matters is being organized and knowing how to prioritize your life matters.

2. Carry out daily reviews

Another excellent way to avoid procrastination is through daily reviews. If you allocate ten minutes from your day, you can assess how things are going. When you are doing the review, you will be able to find the priorities of your day. Then, you can analyze the tasks that will have a huge impact on your short-term goals. To make this review session simpler, consider carrying out a Q&A format. What are the scheduled meetings that you need to attend? Are there any emails that you must reply to today? Are there any documents that need to be edited today? Are there any appointments that will take more time than you allocated? What are the tasks that require more attention?

Likewise, you should do a Q&A to find out the layout of the day. But you don't have to stick to the questions that I have mentioned. Instead, you can prepare your own Q&A and follow it. If you do this daily review, you will be able to understand the layout for the day. When you have your layout, you will be able to stay on the track. You will have proper knowledge of the tasks that need more time or a quick response. Hence, you will not procrastinate because you are aware that it will impact your goals negatively.

If you want to know one of the best concepts that beat procrastination, it is the Pareto Principle. This is all about an 80/20 rule. Try to learn more about this concept before you apply it to your day-to-day activities.

3. MIT's or the Most Important Tasks

It's tough to beat procrastination if you begin your day with a to-do-list that bursts with tasks. You must have a simplified to-do-list if you want to get things done on time and correctly. How can you simplify your to-do-list? It is pretty simple if you focus on MIT's - most important tasks. You have to settle for the tasks that will have a considerable impact on your long-term goals. This is recommended by many experts who focus on productivity.

My tips are to select the top three important tasks that need to be handled by the end of the day. It is better to pick two important tasks that have tight deadlines and another that will impact your long-term career goal. If you keep an eye on MIT's concept, you will be able to curb procrastination. Once you complete the two most important activities, you will be interested in doing the other activities by the end of the day. And that motivation is very much needed if you want to succeed in beating procrastination.

4. The Eisenhower Matrix

Who doesn't like productivity? Who isn't glad when things happen the way they were planned? But sometimes, things don't work as you planned. If your life is anything like mine, filled with constant emergencies and changes, you must have the ability to make quick decisions.

If you want to make a quick decision, you need the support from the Eisenhower Matrix. The founder of this concept, Dwight Davis Eisenhower, was a general in the army. It was the reason why he invented this concept. It's not always possible to work according to the plan when you are in an army. There will be sudden and important changes. In such an instance, the Eisenhower Matrix concept was the guideline.

If Eisenhower utilized this in the army, there is no reason why we can't utilize this in our lives to avoid procrastination! When you are dealing with this concept, you shouldn't forget the four quadrants related to it. By focusing on the four quadrants, you will be able to approach your day-to-day tasks accordingly. Let me mention the four quadrants in detail:

Quadrant 1: Urgent plus important

These are the tasks that need to be completed first because they are way more important than any other tasks and they directly deal with your career goals. Plus, you must complete the tasks right away because they are urgent. If you complete these tasks, you will be able to avoid negative consequences. Once you get your Q1 tasks completed, you will be able to focus on other tasks. For example, if you have to submit a project by the end of the day, your complete attention should be given to that project because it is both urgent and important.

Quadrant 2: Important yet not urgent

The tasks under Q2 are important, but they are not urgent. Even though they might have a huge impact, they are not as time sensitive as Q1. Compare Q2 to Q1, and then, you will understand the difference clearly. Typically, Q2 tasks will include the ones that have a huge impact on your long-term career or life goals. Yes, you need to allocate more time and attention to these tasks. But you seldom do it because your mind knows that the tasks in Q2 can wait.

Meanwhile, you'll be focused on the tasks in other quadrants. Don't make this mistake because your long-term goals are the reasons why your short-term goals exist. For example, your health is one of the important factors, so if you don't spend enough time on it, you will regret it. Yet, when you get busy, you are unlikely to spend time on Q2 tasks. Especially, you are not obliged to answer to anyone about Q2 tasks.

Quadrant 3: Urgent yet not important

The tasks under Q3 are urgent, but you don't necessarily have to spend your time on them. You can either automate or delegate tasks to someone who can handle the work. These tasks are not so important, so it is okay to delegate them. These tasks often come from a third party and the tasks under Q3 will not have a direct influence on your career goals. But when you are handling Q3 tasks, you must note down the tasks that you delegate. For example, if you are working on a time-sensitive project and the phone rings, you might get distracted answering it. Or sometimes, it might not even be an important call. For such activities, you can assign someone. Even if it's an urgent call, you can still assign it to a person who can handle it. Through this, you will be able to manage your day!

Quadrant 4: Not important plus not urgent

The tasks under Q4 include the tasks that need to be avoided. These tasks waste your time unnecessarily. If you don't spend ANY time on Q4 tasks, you will be able to spend more time on the tasks under Q2. By now, you'll know what Q4 tasks consist of. Anyway, they are activities like watching TV, surfing the Internet, playing games, and much more. So, should you eliminate Q4? Well, no! You shouldn't. If you don't have a balanced lifestyle, you might even struggle to protect your job.

Habits of People with Mental Toughness

All mentally tough people have developed specific characteristics that are helpful to how they think, react, and make important decisions. Studying these characteristics and making attempts to mimic the behaviors and thinking patterns is one sure way to reach your goal of mental toughness faster. Use it as a blueprint that can be used and reused at will. Over time, the process will become like second nature. You will instantly know when you are falling back into old habits or behaviors and can correct the course.

Ability to Make Non-Emotional Choices

Allowing an emotional state to dictate your decision-making process will skew your outcome in directions that are non-productive or harmful. No matter how much your small child wants to cross a busy street by themselves and offer a tantrum to try and force a decision in their favor, better sense usually prevails, and the child waits until a responsible person can help them navigate heavy traffic safely. Letting emotions drive the decision can have terrible consequences, depending on the situation. Learn to separate emotion from sensible, rational thoughts.

See the reality of the situation

Raw emotions can paint colors onto a canvas, which are not truly a part of the landscape. Irrational fears, negative thoughts, and a generalized feeling of hopelessness can invade every time you are faced with having to make an emotionally laced decision. As difficult as it may seem, take time to calmly look at the situation with an eye for realism.

Goal-Driven

Keeping your eye on the goal is an important part of the development of mental toughness and a standard characteristic of anyone that always seems to achieve everything they set out to do or attain. It is an admirable quality worth replicating as often as possible.

Recognizing a dead-end road

Taking the wrong path or making incorrect decisions is a waste of valuable time, resources, and energy. The skills it takes to recognize a dead-end road before you take the plunge is priceless. Is it a road filled with potholes or other unsavory obstacles? Is there a smoother, more direct route available? Not every path in life need be a struggle. At times, the struggles experienced are due to poor decision-making. Step back and look at the big picture. Even a difficult hedge-maze is solvable by looking at it from above.

Untethering from details

Details can keep you bogged down, much like the tethers that hold back a hot air balloon from its flight. It is important to address all the details but do not get hung up in the process. Keep pushing forward for positive results. Maintain flexibility to change things if it makes the process easier. Higher levels of success are possible if you refrain from boxing yourself into side compartments and hop down unnecessary rabbit holes. Keep your eye on the goal line.

Keeping a finished vision in mind

Knowing you have completed a road trip is obvious once you have reached your desired destination. An important characteristic of those with mental toughness is the ability to keep the finished goal or vision in mind, no matter what mayhem and chaos happens. It sounds easier than when you are stuck in the situation. The skill of practically putting on blinders to avoid being affected by the emotions of others is one that will serve you well. Stay in the knowledge that reaching your goal often means making unpleasant decisions or ones that are not popular with everyone in your circle.

Ability to Set Aside Stress and Emotion

Stress can get kicked into high gear during emotional situations and exchanges. Decision-making and solutions can become clouded when stress is in a peak amount. Become instantly tougher in mental processes by learning how to set stress and emotional entanglement aside. You need a clearing, devoid of pressure to have the best perspective on any given situation.

Ability to Welcome Change and Remain Flexible

When companies downsize or restructure, employees are faced with job loss, and this can sometimes be devastating. A mentally strong person will seize the opportunity to improve their life by weighing all of their options. If a mentally strong person who had been considering a career change is suddenly faced with losing their job, he or she will take this time to develop their skill set, return to school, or polish their resume to make a career change.

Refuse to Let Fear Hold Them Back

A mentally tough person does not let fear hold them back. Everyone must go through challenges in life, and it is how we view those challenges that can shape our lives for the better. Change is scary, but so is remaining in the same stagnant situation indefinitely. A mentally tough person would rather be scared for a short amount of time while they are going through a change in life than live in fear of the change, never improving or bettering their situation.

Will Not Let Toxic People Affect Them

A toxic person is someone who ruins the environment or the atmosphere for those around them. The toxic person might be incredibly jealous, judgmental, or just negative overall. A toxic person is like the grown-up version of the playground bully: he or she has low self-esteem and is so unhappy with their own lives, so they are constantly trying to bring others down to their level. A mentally strong person realizes this and will do their best to see things from the toxic person's point of view if possible. A mentally strong person also realizes that the toxic person is unhappy, so he or she will not let the toxic opinions and attitude affect them and their work.

Exert Assertiveness

A mentally strong person is assertive. They say what they mean, and they mean what they say. They know how to use concise language so that the meaning of their words is not mistaken, and their intentions are not taken the wrong way. Mentally strong people know how to say no. They know that it's ok to take time to themselves, whether that means saying no to an invitation they don't want to accept or simply staying in on a Saturday night to recharge. Mentally strong people also know when to set boundaries.

They are very confident

If you don't feel confident about yourself and your skills, you cannot expect someone else to feel confident about you. Real confidence is essential and not false bravado. People often tend to mask their insecurities by merely projecting confidence, instead of being confident. A confident person will always stand apart when compared to all those who are indecisive, doubtful, and skittish. Their confidence often inspires others as well.

They are good at neutralizing toxic people

A mentally tough person can keep his or her emotions in check while confronting a toxic person. Their approach would often be rational. If you want to be mentally strong, then you should be able to identify negative emotions like anger and shouldn't let these feelings get the better of you.

They can say no

If you want to reduce your chances of experiencing stress and depression, then learn to say "no." Saying "no" is, in fact, good for your mental health. All those who are mentally tough possess the self-esteem and the foresight that helps them say no. If you have trouble saying "no" to others, then you should start working on it immediately. Saying "no" not only helps you in avowing unnecessary burden, but it will also help you in prioritizing your work and cutting off toxic people from your life.

They can embrace failure

Failures are very common, and everyone has their fair share of failures in their lives. Mentally tough people are capable of embracing their failures. No one can experience success without knowing what failure is. When you can acknowledge that you are on the wrong path, are aware of the mistakes you are making, and can embrace your failures, only then will you be able to achieve success.

They exercise

Exercising can help you in finding mental, physical, and emotional stability. When you start exercising, you are not only improving your physical health, you are getting rid of negative emotions as well. Start exercising at least thrice a week and you will feel better about yourself. Your self-esteem will get a healthy boost when you can develop your physical image. A person who is mentally tough knows the importance of exercising and will make sure that they are getting their quota of exercise daily. The endorphin high that you experience after exercising can lend your perspective some much-needed positivity.

They get sufficient sleep

Sleep is quite essential if you are trying to improve your mental toughness. While you are sleeping, your brain starts working on removing all the toxic proteins that are produced because of the neural activity that takes place while you are awake. Well, your brain can do this only when you are asleep.

They are always positive

Reading news these days has become a sad affair. Mass killings, suicide bombings, violence, crippling economies, failing companies, and plenty of environmental mishaps. Phew, that is a lot of negativity to go through. In times like these, it is quite easy to give up on a positive attitude. A mentally tough person wouldn't worry about all that for a simple reason. He or she cannot control any of those things. However, their attitude is something that they can control, and that's what they would concentrate on. They wouldn't waste their energies on something that cannot be helped. Instead, try utilizing your energy to do something good, and it might be helpful.

Mental toughness isn't a quality that only a few are blessed with. You can achieve it with some effort.

Decide to Change Your Behaviors

Be a Better Person

To change your life, you must also learn how to become a better person.

Making the most out of your life requires both external and internal changes. Although you can schedule your time properly and start implementing good habits, it won't have as much of an effect if you don't change the person that you are. It's important to be positive, as this can have a huge effect on how you feel. You may view yourself in a better light, and others will appreciate you more for it. Being a better person is more than just being nice to others. It involves kindness to both yourself and others. It's important to treat yourself well so that you can practice positivity and have a greater appreciation for yourself. Practicing self-compassion is important for you to be happy, and you can't treat others well until you learn how to treat yourself well. Patience is also very important to learn. You must be patient with yourself, as everything will take time. The skills that you've learned from this book will take time to affect you; there won't be immediate results. Patience can help you to stay motivated even when things don't go to plan. Being an understanding of both yourself and others is also crucial. Everyone makes mistakes. You must learn to forgive others for their mistakes, as holding a grudge will not get you anywhere. Additionally, you may learn how to not overreact to everything. You may choose to simply respond.

Kindness and Compassion

Kindness and compassion are crucial to becoming a better person. They can both help you to increase your positivity. You may practice both of them towards yourself and others, and it can really help you to be happier. When you learn to treat yourself better, you'll understand how to treat others better. Living a life full of kindness and compassion can help you to spread more joy and positivity. You will rid yourself of negativity and learn to be selfless. However, that doesn't mean that you won't take care of yourself. You may practice both of these toward yourself.

Kindness is so important. It's also really easy! You can take just a few seconds to be kinder. Using your manners is a great way to treat others with kindness. By simply thanking others for what they do, you can make someone's day better. It's always nice to know when what you do is appreciated. We often forget to thank others, and kindness overall may be something that is neglected. It's important to take a few moments to make others' days brighter. You may also simply smile at others. Don't forget that strangers are people, too. It's hard to truly be kind and genuine if you seem cold and unfriendly on the outside. Typically, your outward actions reflect how you're feeling on the inside. A simple smile can help you to not only seem kind but feel better about yourself. Don't get discouraged if others don't smile back; they probably aren't used to it. But you could make someone's day so much better just from a smile.

You may help others out or volunteer. This could mean giving someone your spare change or making them a health pack (with toothpaste, toothbrush, etc.).

This might mean volunteering somewhere or even just picking up some litter that you see. Regardless, you can make the world a better place with some random acts of kindness. You can visit a nursing home, send cards to those in the military, or thank someone for their work. You might consider paying for the person behind you in line or letting people ahead of you in line.

Another way to express kindness is by checking in with those who you already know. You may send them a card, call them up, or pay them a visit. Maybe you can bake some cookies and give them to people in your life. Remember to appreciate the people in your life.

Additionally, you should express self-compassion. This is so important for making yourself happy and taking care of yourself. With a little push, it's easy to help others, be more understanding with them, and forgive them when they've made a mistake. However, it may be a bit harder for you to do the same for yourself. You may dismiss taking care of yourself and put every other person first. It can be hard to forgive yourself for making mistakes, and you may not understand with yourself when you make mistakes.

To practice self-compassion, you may take a few steps to take care of yourself. Practicing mindfulness can help you to bring yourself back to the present. Instead of dwelling on past mistakes that you've made or being nervous about your future, you can focus on what's happening at this moment. You may also remember that everybody makes mistakes. When you make a mistake, you are likely to be the one who is the hardest on yourself. Acknowledge the mistake and learn from it. You can do better in the future. Holding onto and dwelling on the mistake will not change it or make it any better. You must become okay with imperfection. There will always be more to learn, more ways to grow, and different ways to improve you. Don't stop trying to make progress but accept that you will never be completely perfect. That's okay that you won't be.

Patience

Patience is very important in life. There will be many times where you will have to wait. You must wait for others. You must keep going and wait for your hard work to pay off. It's important to practice patience in all areas of your life. It can make you a much stronger person, and you'll be happier for it. These days, everything must be done immediately. With technology, we can have instant gratification. You can instantly search on your phone for information and get it immediately. When something takes more than a few moments, we start to panic. By practicing patience, you may be able to focus your attention for longer instead of needing everything done immediately.

You can practice patience; it is actually a great skill to master. One easy way to do so is by making yourself wait. Become comfortable with boredom. We're so scared of being bored that we will look for anything to do to occupy our time. If you can take a moment to simply relax, you will feel much better. Practice your self-control every so often and make yourself wait. This may be as simple as taking a few moments to breathe before eating. You can build up how long you wait and what you wait for.

You may eliminate the activities that make you impatient in the first place. If there's something you do that sucks up a lot of your time but isn't fulfilling, cut it out or alter it. This may require you to switch up your schedule and make it so that you don't have to be so impatient. If you feel impatient when faced with traffic, leave your house earlier so that you don't have to have this problem in the first place.

Start to feel more comfortable with waiting. When you start feeling impatient, ask yourself why that is. Are you bored? Are you nervous that you won't get something done on time? Take things one step at a time and relax. This may require you to take deep breaths while counting to ten. Ask yourself what is causing your frustration and what the solution is to it. There's almost always a solution to our problems, yet we fail to take the time to look for them. Focus on one thought at a time and figure out what your best course of action is for any problems.

If you must, have some go-to ideas for when you're feeling impatient. Sometimes, you may feel impatient but don't want to start on something. You may have a person come over that's late. You feel impatient, yet you don't want to get into anything deep in case they arrive. Have some small activities to keep yourself occupied when these situations occur. For some, this may be a book or magazine to flip through. For others, it may be a game on your phone or something similar. Figure out a way to calm yourself down when you're feeling a bit impatient.

Understanding

Being more understanding is a great skill to learn. When you understand, it doesn't mean that you support any mistakes. You aren't agreeing with anything. You simply understand. This is a great way to combat perfectionism and cut yourself some slack. You won't always be perfect, and neither will anybody else. It's important to remember that although you should always strive to improve yourself and work hard, you must also understand that there are times where it's okay to cut yourself some slack. If you're running your first marathon, it would be pretty crazy for you to finish in the first place. You must understand that it takes practice; the winner has probably spent years training and competing.

When others don't behave the way that we think they're supposed to, we often get upset. We may be mad at them for seemingly ruining our plans. They may disappoint us, and we wish that they were different. However, you can't think like this. Everybody has their own goals and opinions. If everyone lived their lives just for you, there wouldn't be any excitement in life. Plans will always change, and things happen. You need to be able to understand that everyone makes mistakes.

To be more understanding of others, you may do a few things. One way to be more understanding is to stop judging others so much. Instead of judging their actions, understand them, and really make an effort to hear their side of the story. Don't argue with the person or try to rub it in that they've messed up. Really listen to them and understand fully what they're saying. We are often only half-listen and think about our own thoughts instead. Learning to understand others can really help you to strengthen your relationships and be much happier in life. You won't be so uptight about everything, and it will be harder to get upset.

It's just as important, if not more important, to understand yourself. Understand yourself when you've made a mistake. Understand yourself when you don't achieve something or aren't perfect. Understand yourself when your mood is down. There are so many ways that you can understand yourself. When you can practice understanding others and yourself, you'll feel much better. It won't seem as awful when something small goes wrong. You won't feel the need to beat yourself up for a little mistake that you made. It won't help you at all to do this. What will help is acknowledging that something went wrong and moving on from it. This is the greatest help to you. It will really make a difference in your life.

The next time that you feel the need to beat yourself up, especially over something small, pause for a moment. Consider how it will really help you to solve the problem. It won't. Acknowledge any thoughts you have about this and push them away. Instead, focus on how you can be better in the future and what you can do right now to solve any problems that you may have.

Set Realistic Goals for Personal Growth

Do you know that the power to change your life is buried within you? This power can be unleashed at any time, and it has been used by successful people. Power is the ability to visualize or the potential to visualize your goal. The important part of it is the ability to see your goal and that you are more likely to achieve. What could be that one thing you have always wished to have? If you can set a goal, then you are going to make it happen. The drive to achieve whatever you have desired is the goal that you have set. When the goal setting is applied well with the right intentions and the right momentum, then you will move from where you are now to where you want to be. You need to have it at the back of your mind that where you want to move to always start with your vision.

What is the power of visualizing your goals? If you want to increase your chances of getting to your goals, then you should start visualizing them. When you can visualize, then you will only need to do some important things as well. It starts with teaching your brain to know the kind of resources it will need to get to your goals. Having an inner motivation that will push you to strive for your dreams and goals. Always think positively which will help you to be on track and achieve success in the long run. How to visualize your goals is a simple step of finding a quiet place where you can sit and with no interruptions. All you need to do is to get comfortable and let your mind do its work.

Do you know that athletes also use the method of visualization? They don't just wake up one day and start doing their practice without any set goal and where they see themselves after they are through with their training. They use visualization all the time to better their performance.

The reasons why visualization work is that our brains are wired, the neurons in our mind will interpret images into reality. When you visualize on doing things, you will command your body to create pathways and memories of how to act on the action even though you may not act. The more times you visualize, the more you make your mind to perfect on the mental aspect before the physical.

How to Visualize Your Goals

Have a vision and a goal, and the vision should not something new but something that is already in existence. Vision acts as a big picture of what you desire to have. Goals are just milestones that requires completion. A goal is simply a steppingstone that you will meet on the way to your ultimate destination. There are key aspects that you need to be aware of when using visualization as a method to help you achieve your goals.

The power of imagination makes us infinite.

John Muir

Focusing on the Senses

For example, when you get to visualize about your dream house there is that mental picture you will create in your mind, it is early in the morning, and you are sited at the yard, which has the beautiful flowers, you can even smell the rose flowers and other flowers, you can hear the birds chirping in the next tree. All these experiences will help you to visualize, but you may not be in a position to use all your senses.

Focusing on the Details

This means taking focus to the next level. When we are talking about in detail is that you get to focus on the specific information. The only way you will focus on the details is by looking at the specific things carefully for a few minutes.

Doing Away with Distractions

When you are visualizing something, you should not get distracted. When you don't want to be distracted, get a silent room, then switch off your phone, as it will allow you to focus more on what matters. This will happen mostly occur when you are just getting started, but the moment you set your mind to visualizing success, then the noise from the background won't bother you.

Never Give Up

If you want to be an expert, then no matter what comes your way, you need to hold on and never allow it to stop you from moving forward. Visualizing isn't something easy to do; at first, you may fail, but with more practice, you meet success on your way. At some point, you will not realize the success you have made, but when you look back, you will see how far you have come.

Tips for those who want to practice visualization for the first time. The following exercises will help you practice and become a better person in visualizing your goals. The first thing to do is look at colors. Look for a page with many colors and study the colors then close your eyes. After that, try to picture the colors, you will realize that for the first time, the colors in your mind will fade away, but when you proceed to do it for maybe 3 times, then you will visualize the colors well.

Importance of Visualizing your Goals

Everyone at the end of the day wants to be successful, so if you make it a habit to visualize success, then you are destined for greatness. This doesn't happen when you sit back and daydream or fantasizing about your life magically. You will get there, no, you need to get the right tools and work towards your goals, visualization work alongside hard work, having good people who will push you to work for what you want to achieve.

Using the visualization method will help you to achieve your goals. It may not happen immediately, but with patience and determination, you will see it happening. The only encouragement is that if you can start to visualize your goals, then in the future, you will see the progress that you will have made.

How SMART is your Goal?

Anyone who has had experienced management at some point came across the word SMART.

But what is SMART to the ordinary Joe anyway?

Well, SMART is an acronym taken as a principle behind success. Whatever it is we are working on; it has to be SMART. It has to have the essential qualities that indicate quality work and dedication to a perceived goal.

Now, let us dissect and discover what SMART actually means.

1. Specific

Let us face the fact that we need to focus on the things that matter. Whether preparing a project for work or realizing a personal work, we need to put in our minds the thing we want to pursue. Why follow a map when there is no telling what it is you are looking for?

In many cases, people tend to act rather than make clear the very idea they want to realize. This leads them to a fruitless quest for nothing. It is very unfortunate for some to exert so much effort only to be dissatisfied in the end. Nothing really matters when for a fact they do; it is just a matter of directing your attention to the concept in your head. When making a plan, try to think about the objectives you want to achieve. Think about it first; going about it will follow.

2. Measurable

For a fact, plans should have a measurable character. What this means is that you need a type of metric to know how much you are progressing and how much you are regressing.

Not all plans end up as intended. For instance, when starting up a business, you need to understand that there are variables involved across various aspects in managing a business. You need to calculate your operating expenses against your net profits. You also need to figure out the best marketing techniques to attract customers. And you also need to track the growth of the business over the course of time. This allows you to some measure of control with how your plan or idea is catching on, enabling you to see what is wrong with it and implement the proper solutions for improving it.

Measurability is thus crucial if you want to see the success of a plan or idea through.

3. Achievable

In all aspects of realizing an important idea or concept, you need to gauge how much of an attainable endeavor it would be

For instance, an idea of a useful and marketable product hits you, and you set about drawing it from the mind and into the real world. Usually, you would employ numerous devices that can help you in achieving it. So, you filter out what works best from those that won't work at all.

However, there will be times that nothing seems to come close to a viable solution to achieving the idea. In this case, the problem does not lie with the selection of the strategies but with the idea itself. Consequently, you will be led towards modifying the idea and make it more in tune with certain limits.

And that is precisely the gist of this principle. You can learn from the age-old mantra, "Know thyself; know thy limits."

4. Realistic

Aside from knowing what would be achieved in pursuing a plan, you need to know whether or not it will ever see the light of day. More importantly, you need to know if it would indeed be an endeavor that can be sustained in the long run.

Realism is vital. Managers understand this because no plan or proposition or an idea in the history of human endeavor has ever been perfect. There will be flaws and, in the most crucial aspects, there will be real-world factors and obstacles. We need to acknowledge the fact plans are not always perfect in every way, so we need to modify and change them according to how much we can achieve. We need to ground them on realistic soil.

5. Time-bound

Planning, in some respects, has to adhere to a timetable. Notwithstanding the importance of emphasizing quality and measurability, we also need to understand that a plan has a shelf life. They have a specific target date to be accomplished.

A project does not have any serious inclination towards completing itself when the people behind it lack a deadline which motivates them. Aside from the fact that it oversees the completion of a project, a timetable also ensures that it follows through a specific, step-by-step path towards realization. We simply could not make a rush job out of a significant endeavor such as a book or an invention. We could not even afford to procrastinate and put off important work because "inspiration comes in batches." We must understand that we need to be more organized in terms of using time as a vital element to see a project through.

With SMART in mind, you need to develop a keen sense of finding minute details about your idea. Then, using the criteria, check whether the idea is in line with each individual rubric, once it satisfies these indicators, then you can be sure that the idea would be closer to reality.

The path to self-discipline is never just about motivational posters and self-help books. It is more about using the current material and mental resources you have to make the concepts in your head come to life.

So, before you linger on the kind of results you want to achieve, start first by analyzing what to do and what should be done to make something that is useful and efficient. Using the SMART model, you will become wiser in making crucial decisions for rousing you to action and, in effect, making a difference.

How to Choose the Best Course of Action

Identify your #1 Master Goal

You have identified the three goals you feel most passionate about. From that short list, identify the one goal that means the most to you. It is the one thing; above all else, you desire to have. This should be easy because chances are, you already know what it is. The other two goals are important, but you will want to focus here on one goal first.

It is the one goal that will impact your life in substantial ways. This is designed to break you out of your mold and make the unimaginable come true. It is everything you have ever dreamed of doing and becoming.

Your #1 Master Goal has to be the one thing in life you have always desired the most. It is your grandest adventure, a seemingly insurmountable obstacle that scares you as much as it excites you. It brings everything in your life into direct alignment with the great purpose that governs all things.

Action task: Write down your #1 Master Goal. Why is this your biggest goal? How will it impact your life and the lives of others when it is realized?

Expand on action tasks for Master Goal #1.

The final step is to break each action task into smaller steps, so they are easier to tackle. By breaking them down, you are giving yourself manageable chunks to work with, while reducing stress.

By breaking down the goal into sizeable chunks, it will be easier to track your success.

These smaller steps could include making phone calls, arranging a meeting, or doing research on a subject.

Expand on the action tasks for your #1 goal. Go back to the mind-mapping strategy and write down as many tasks as you can think of—even if they are months away.

Action task: Make a list of action tasks for your #1 Master Goal.

Organize your plan into priority action steps.

Now that you have your list of action tasks, put these in order of importance. What needs to be done today? This week? Within the next three months?

Take five minutes every night before bedtime to write down the one task you will complete the following day. This is a powerful habit. By doing one thing every day, it pushes your goal closer to the finish line.

Taking massive action really means acting consistently, so every day, you must do something that moves the needle.

Action task: Prioritize your action steps.

Identify the barriers blocking your progress

As with anything, there will be challenges and obstacles to work through. Identify three immediate challenges you will encounter while working towards your goals. This usually comes down to one of three things—or, it could be all three:

1. You lack information. Is there anything you need to know to move ahead? Do you need to take a course, do an interview, or call somebody?

2. A lack of resources. You might need something such as money to continue your goal, but remember, you are limited not by resources but a lack of resourcefulness. This means you can find a way to make it work and get more money. Maybe you need to convince someone to help you, such as a mentor or coach.

3. Your values are confused. There are times when our values are not in alignment with the goals we are pursuing. This requires us to evaluate the values driving us.

Whatever barriers are in our way, there is a way to get through it. Work out the solutions and create an action plan to chip away at the weaknesses.

Action task: Identify the barriers that could hold you back.

Review Your Progress

This is probably the most vital step to effectively manage your goal portfolio. By reviewing your goals on a regular basis, you can easily recognize and monitor your progress. During the review process, you will:

- Identify pending obstacles blocking your path.

- Review and update your action checklist of tasks required to achieve your goal(s):

- Assess your progress and consider whether your deadline is manageable; and

- Add any new thoughts or ideas to support your continued progress.

It is easy to get pulled away from the work you really want to do, but most of our distractions can be managed easily. The reason is most distractions are self-created. Of course, you will always have family situations come up, or a friend drop by who needs something. This is where blocking off time each day to get your work done and put time into your project is critical.

One major distraction many people have is negative or fragmented thinking. Our mind wants to do one thing, while our will wants to do another.

This is when concentration comes into play. When you concentrate on something, you make it your most important priority. You focus your energy on the task, and then concentrate to make sure it is done correctly, and you are doing only those things required to move closer to your goals.

Action task: Review the progress you are making once a week. Take note of the areas in which you are failing and try to tighten them up.

Goal Builder's Checklist:

o   Commit your goal to paper. Write a brief statement about the goal.

o   Create a working list of steps necessary to achieve this goal.

o   Visualize the goal coming true.

o   Create a deadline.

o   Place the goal into a category.

o   Define the desired result(s) of achieving your goals.

o   Monitor and track your progress.

o   Review your progress.

o   Revise your goals on a regular basis.

o   Describe the expected life impact of achieving your goals.

o   Describe who you will become after achieving a lifelong goal of significant importance.

Tiny Milestones and Celebrating Small Achievements

Goals can be deceiving. You might have goals for yourself, but are they too big? Do you feel overwhelmed when you look over your goals, thinking, "How am I going to do this?" I know how you feel. My goals are big, as well, and while there is nothing wrong with shooting for the moon, we can get frustrated if we are working on the same thing a year from now and feel as if we are getting nowhere.

Progress is measured best when it is in small chunks. This means setting small goalposts for yourself that are easy to measure.

Take this book, for example.

When I started writing it, I knew it would be about 50K words. That is a lot of writing. Feeling pressured to get it done in two months,

At the end of the day, I could tick off whether I had finished a certain word count or not. Building small milestones into your projects, hobbies, or work is a sure-fire way to stay on track. Every day you are working on this is a day closer to your goal.

I'll give you another example: When I started working out again, I had a goal to be able to do 50 push-ups in one session. That is a lot. So, I started out by doing just five the first day. Then, every day after that, I increased the push-ups by just one. Yes, only one—but after two weeks, I was doing 20 a day. After a month, I was able to do 35-40.

I would have given up without this mini-milestone formula, but by increasing your performance by just 1%, you can make tremendous gains over time. You will hit your target and finish what you set out to do.

How do you set up tiny milestones? Take your goal and break it into the smallest chunks possible. Even if it seems ridiculously tiny, this is better than doing nothing. A 1% improvement is better than 0% any day. If you do nothing, you get nothing, but do one small action, and within two or three weeks, you will see the results you made. If you have been in the habit of giving up on things you love in the past, this could be prevented from now on, if you do the smallest thing possible.

Here is another example: Playing the guitar. Did you know that most of the best songs were created with just three chords? If you spent 80% of your time mastering these three chords, you could play a lot of music.

One of the better reasons small goals work is they remove the overwhelming thought that we must know everything about our passion, if we want to be good at it.

If this were the case, you'd quit after a few months. It takes a lifetime to master anything. That goes for writing books or playing music or sports. We can always be better at something—no matter how good we already are.

Jerry Seinfeld—one of the greatest comedians of our time—still does stand-up comedy to stay sharp. He has $700M and isn't doing it for the money. He remembers when he was a struggling comedian, and how important it was to stay on top of his game.

The tiny milestone strategy is so basic that many people overlook it. They think they have to do more, know everything, and do it perfectly before they can consider themselves to be experts. I'll tell you how to stop giving up on everything: Do a little bit each day. Set your mini goal for the week. Then, keep hitting that mini goal each day.

If you focus on developing tiny milestones, here is what you could get done in six months:

- If you write 300 words a day, you'll have written a book.

- Practice the major three chords on a guitar, and you'll be playing songs at parties: and

- Save $5 a day instead of going to Starbucks, and you'll have $1,825 saved in the bank within the first year.

I know lots of people (myself included) who gave up on saving money. They said it was too difficult to keep money in the bank, but they were giving up on the wrong thing. Instead of giving up daily trips to the coffee shop or buying crap they didn't need, they made a decision that saving was difficult and threw in the towel. They continued those habits, throwing away thousands of dollars a year.

However, another friend gave up a few habits, decided achieving his goal of saving $5K a year was more important, and sacked away $400 a month for 12 months. How? Saving a tiny amount every day. Just like you can play an instrument or learn a language by taking it in tiny sessions a day, you can save money, lose weight, or learn a new language, too.

Tiny milestones are easy to manage. You are much less likely to give up on something if you can see your progress happening daily.

Setting up your tiny milestones is easy, too. I'll walk you through a simple, step-by-step process:

1. Write down your #1 goal. Is it losing weight? Writing a book? Decluttering your apartment?

2. Make a list of action steps for each of your tiny milestones. This should only be three for each milestone.

3. Review your progress every week. Do this at the end of the week.

4. Celebrate your big win. Too often, we take goals for granted. You don't have to achieve something amazing to earn your right to celebrate. Every small task completed is a step toward reaching your outcome.

5. Focus on the action and not the overall big picture. In other words, if your goal is to run a marathon, you will have to run often to condition yourself. So just run a few kilometers at a time—or, just one kilometer at a time, if that is all you can handle.

Build these tiny milestones into your daily habits. The consistency of our actions gets us where we want to be.

Conclusion

T hank you for making it to the end of "Rewire your brain. Build mental toughness, train your brain to increase willpower", in this book, I have provided you with a considerable wealth of information and advice to help you kick your negative outlook, your negative self-talk, your inner critic, whatever you want to call it. We've looked at how to start believing in yourself and how to always choose yourself.

If you've read this book from cover-to-cover, you now know just how destructive negative thinking can be to your emotions, your health. To change your life, you must also learn how to become a better person. Making the most out of your life requires both external and internal changes. Although you can schedule your time properly and start implementing good habits, it won't have as much of an effect if you don't change the person that you are. It's important to be positive, as this can have a huge effect on how you feel. You may view yourself in a better light, and others will appreciate you more for it. Being a better person is more than just being nice to others.

Remember that self-discipline is a skill - one that can be learned like riding a bike. Learn self-discipline as if you're trying to learn to ride a bike or swim in the ocean – it takes time to cultivate the skill. If you don't know how to swim, how do you start? You dip in the water and start practicing. Then you stay afloat for a while and repeat until you can swim. You build the momentum to practice more until you're a swimmer. Self-discipline is based on 2 things: daily practice and momentum. To obtain self-discipline, a person has to hone their skills to build consistency and small step their way until they've mastered the skill.

Also, problems often seem like negative things are life; if you never faced any challenges in your life, how would you be able to grow and embrace all of the changes that life has to offer you? No one enjoys it's coming up against the problem. If you feel like you are alone on this, know that you are not. But believe it or not, problems can bring benefits. There are a number of ways that problems and challenges affect us in a positive way. Let's explore some of those reasons. During the struggle, even though you may not feel it, you are getting stronger. Problems allow you to learn resilience and stamina. By remaining steadfast during a challenging situation, you are growing who you are.

Lastly, remember that all mentally tough people have developed specific characteristics that are helpful to how they think, react, and make important decisions. Studying these characteristics and making attempts to mimic the behaviors and thinking patterns is one sure way to reach your goal of mental toughness faster. If you follow this book and this advice, you'll be amazed at the difference it will make in your life. You'll feel like a better you; you'll achieve more and feel great. Good luck.

Thank you for purchasing and reading this book. Feel free to leave a favorable review.

CPSIA information can be obtained
at www.ICGtesting.com
Printed in the USA
BVHW061555300321
603714BV00009B/637